A GUIDE DOG
GOES TO SCHOOL

Also by Elizabeth Simpson Smith

A Dolphin Goes to School:
The Story of Squirt, a Trained Dolphin

A GUIDE DOG GOES TO SCHOOL

The Story of a Dog Trained to Lead the Blind

Elizabeth Simpson Smith
Illustrated by Bert Dodson

William Morrow and Company, Inc. / New York

Library of Congress Cataloging-in-Publication Data

Smith, Elizabeth Simpson.
A guide dog goes to school.

Includes index.
Summary: Follows a puppy as she goes through the stages
of training to become a guide dog for a blind person.
1. Guide dogs—Training of—Juvenile literature.
[1. Guide dogs] I. Dodson, Bert. II. Title.
HV1780.2.S65   1987   362.4'183   87-11056
ISBN 0-688-06844-8
ISBN 0-688-06846-4 (lib. bdg.)

This book is dedicated to Belveia Benzenhafer and Marillyn N. Maxson and their guide dogs, Cinderella and Fraula, with admiration.

ACKNOWLEDGMENTS

The author sincerely thanks Belveia Benzenhafer and Marillyn Maxson for sharing their guide-dog experiences and for verifying the information in the manuscript; Jennifer Bassing and Russell B. Post of Guide Dogs for the Blind, Inc., San Rafael, California, for supplying information and for checking the manuscript for accuracy; Carolyn Goodwin of the 4-H Clubs of America, Lincolnton, North Carolina, for information regarding the organization; and the East Lincoln Animal Hospital, Denver, North Carolina, for information concerning golden retrievers.

CONTENTS

Guide Dogs and
    Guide-Dog Schools   1

One   A Pup Is Born   7

Two   Socializing with a 4-H Family   13

Three   Starting School   20

Four   Meeting a Blind Master   31

Five   Graduation   41

Six   A New Life   44

A Special Message   47

Index   49

GUIDE DOGS AND GUIDE-DOG SCHOOLS

Cinderella is a golden retriever. If you were to visit her at the home where she lives, she would seem just like any other fine dog. You might find her snoozing by the fire or sitting beside her master's chair. Or on a nice day she might be playing in the yard.

But if you were to see Cinderella on the street, she would appear quite different. She would be wearing a harness and leading her master. She would pause at corners to wait for the traffic to clear. But she would not look at you or give you a chance to pet her, for she would be hard at work. Cinderella is a guide dog for the blind.

The idea of using a dog to lead the blind came about in an interesting way. In 1914, during World War One,

the Germans began using German shepherd dogs to carry messages to the front line where actual fighting was taking place. In the process they discovered an amazing thing. The messenger dogs could scent wounded soldiers on the battlefield and lead someone to rescue them. The Germans also discovered that these same dogs could be trained to serve as guides for men who had been blinded during battle. The men then could go outdoors without using a cane or being led by another person.

An American woman named Dorothy Eustis became enthusiastic about this development when she heard of it, and wanted to pursue it further. She thought of the many other blind people who were not able to leave their homes because they did not have anyone to lead them. She decided that dogs should be trained to lead them, too. So with her husband, George Eustis, she set up a training school for guide dogs in Switzerland, where they lived.

Morris Frank was the first person from the United States to get a guide dog from the Eustises' school. With the help of his guide dog, he found he could go to work every day, ride elevators, eat in restaurants, and shop in stores. He was so overjoyed with his new freedom that in 1929 he helped set up the first guide-dog training school in America. It was called The Seeing Eye.

Later, other schools were begun. Now there are a dozen or more training schools throughout the United States where legally blind people may apply for a dog. Each person must be in good health and physically able to take care of a dog. He or she must also have the patience and desire to train at the school. To have a guide dog is a big responsibility and requires maturity. For this reason only people age sixteen and over ordinarily are chosen.

Although it costs thousands of dollars to train a guide dog, blind people are not asked to pay this charge. Usually they pay some small fee, but no suitable blind person is turned away for lack of funds. The schools are nonprofit and are supported by private donations. They receive no money from the government.

German shepherds, Labrador retrievers, and golden retrievers usually are chosen to be guide dogs. These breeds have proved most suitable for they are willing workers, have body coats that are comfortable in both hot and cold climates, and are easy to groom. But other breeds also can be trained. The dog must be tall enough so its master can walk comfortably without stooping, but not so strong that it would unbalance its master.

Each school uses a different name for the dogs it trains, such as Pilot Dogs, Guide Dogs for the Blind, Seeing Eye Dogs, or Leader Dogs. Each school also

uses its own method of training.

Some schools have their own breeding stock living near the campus, while others have in-house breeding programs. When the puppies are about twelve weeks old, they are placed in the care of puppy raisers until they begin formal training.

A dog usually starts school when it is between one and two years old. The training takes three months. Then the dog trains with its blind master for another month.

Although guide dogs are given time off to rest and play, they must work hard every day. Their only pay is praise. But guide dogs appear to lead happy lives. After they have served about ten years, they are old enough to retire. They are returned to the school, where they are taken care of for the rest of their lives. The blind master then gets another guide dog.

This is the story of one guide dog and the way she went to school.

ONE
A PUP IS BORN

Cinderella, a golden retriever, was born one spring evening in the kennels of a guide-dog training school. Her coat was buttery yellow, and her eyes were as brown as walnuts. From the start she seemed destined for a special life. Cinderella was the perkiest and smallest pup in the litter. Her tail twitched happily while she nursed. She romped and played with her brothers and sisters. She even gnawed the breeder's shoelaces when he visited the pen.

Every day she ventured farther from her mother. One day she dived into a mulch pile. Afterward she looked as though she had been playing in cinders. So the breeders named her Cinderella, like the beautiful

girl in the fairy tale. But if she were to become a guide dog, she would be called Cindy while at work. A two-syllable name makes it easier to give and receive commands.

Cinderella was given puppy shots to protect her from diseases. Every week volunteer puppy testers weighed her and charted her growth. They noted that she was friendly and good-natured. This is very important, for an unfriendly and ill-tempered dog would not be a suitable mate for a blind person. Such a dog would be placed in a good home but would not be able to attend school.

"Cinderella is a fine puppy," the testers said. "She may be a good candidate for guide-dog training."

But Cinderella had to pass other tests before the people at the school could be sure. A blind person would be depending on Cinderella for safety, so it was important to know about the dog's natural reflexes. How would she react to loud noises, such as car horns or motorcycle engines? How well would she walk on broken pavement or gravel? Was she jumpy and nervous? What if she chased cats and dogs, pulling her blind master behind her?

When Cinderella was six weeks old, the puppy testers began to test her. They shot off a small pistol behind Cinderella's back. She turned her head sharply and looked in the direction of the pistol, but she didn't yelp, charge, or run away.

Then Cinderella was placed inside a pen with a wire flooring that would feel uncomfortable to her paws. Cinderella tried one foot, then another. Soon she contentedly explored the length of the pen.

Next the testers placed a friendly cat before her, but Cinderella just watched it curiously. They walked her by a mirror, but she only sniffed at her own reflection.

A working guide dog is sure to be bumped and pushed by people on a busy street or in a crowded building. Would Cinderella jump in surprise and throw her master off balance? To find out, the testers tapped and pushed against her side unexpectedly. But Cinderella paid little attention.

For six weeks the testers gave similar tests as they carefully observed Cinderella. She was now twelve weeks old and no longer dependent on her mother for nourishment.

"She has passed every test," they reported. "Now she can be socialized."

Since guide dogs will be living in a home with their blind masters, it is important that they know in advance how to be part of a family. This process is called *socializing*, and it is done by volunteer puppy raisers who live near the guide-dog training school.

Socializing is also an approved project for members of the 4-H Clubs of America, an out-of-school educational organization for boys and girls who want to learn by doing. These puppy raisers are given specific instructions on how to raise a guide dog. The school provides an allowance for dog food and pays all veterinary bills. All the family has to do is provide love and care, and to teach the puppy good manners and basic obedience commands.

"Tomorrow you go off on a new adventure," an instructor said to Cinderella, running his fingers through her thickening fur.

TWO
SOCIALIZING
WITH A 4-H FAMILY

One bright July morning, a van from the school pulled into the Weavers' driveway. Twelve-year-old Benjamin was already waiting, along with his parents and Amy, Benjamin's nine-year-old sister. The instructor stepped from the car, pulled the side door open, and reached for a leash. Out jumped Cinderella, her tail wagging furiously.

"She's yours for a whole year," the instructor told Benjamin. "Remember, no spoiling and no bad habits."

"She's beautiful!" Benjamin cried, picking her up. Cinderella wiggled and lapped his chin with her tongue. Amy and her parents took turns welcoming the new member of their family and asking questions of the instructor.

After good-byes were said, the instructor climbed into the van and started the engine. Nestled in Benjamin's arms, Cinderella watched curiously. As the car backed from the driveway, she gave a little jerk and tried to leap to the ground, but Benjamin held her tightly.

"Don't be scared," he whispered as the van turned into the street and disappeared around the corner. "We'll take good care of you." Cinderella trembled and snuggled against his neck.

They all went indoors, and Benjamin walked Cinderella from room to room. Holding her leash, he let her sniff the strange furniture and soft carpeting. He showed her the padded wicker basket where she would sleep just inside the kitchen door.

Then he led her to a spot in the backyard near Mrs. Weaver's petunia bed. "Good girl," he said when Cinderella relieved herself. Three times every day and once before bedtime, one of the Weavers would take Cinderella to that same spot. In this way she would learn not to mess up the house or the rest of the yard. She would also know not to relieve herself in a neighbor's yard.

That evening Cinderella sniffed at her supper and walked away. "She's homesick," Benjamin announced.

Benjamin heard Cinderella whimpering during the night and knew that she was lonesome. But if he were to put her in his own bed, he would be breaking a rule. Although he could let her sleep in his room, he wanted Cinderella to feel that she belonged to the entire family, not just to him. Eventually the house grew quiet, and Benjamin wondered why. In the morning he found Buttons, the family cat, snuggled next to Cindy. Both were sleeping peacefully.

In the months that followed, Cinderella discovered many new things. She learned the rattle of dishes, the sound of the television, and the ringing of a telephone. She grew accustomed to the flush of a toilet and the ping of a door bell. She knew the smell of food and soap and perfume. She even learned to ignore the cuckoo clock.

Cinderella romped and played with Benjamin, Amy, and their friends. She went with the family on automobile rides and picnics in the park. Mrs. Weaver also took her in the car when she ran errands.

But Cinderella wasn't always good. Sometimes she chased bicycles. Sometimes she made a puddle on the kitchen floor. Sometimes she jumped on furniture and left muddy paw prints. "No, no," Benjamin corrected. When Cinderella misbehaved very badly, such as begging at the table, he scolded her firmly. A blind person certainly could not take a dog that begged into a restaurant or to a friend's house for dinner.

After the scolding, Cinderella's tail drooped and she

stole quietly out of the room. But when she behaved well, Benjamin always praised her lavishly. Then Cinderella's tail would twitch excitedly, and she would go from person to person to be patted and stroked.

Benjamin took Cinderella to obedience training, where she practiced good manners and learned to obey *sit, down, stay,* and *come* commands.

Every few weeks an instructor from the guide-dog school visited the Weavers to check on Cinderella. Benjamin remembered to tell him special things that would be important later.

"She never gets carsick," he said on the instructor's first visit.

"Great," the trainer replied. "She will be able to take her master in cars and buses and taxis. And maybe even airplanes."

When Cinderella was about a year old, the Weavers took her to the guide-dog training school. It was a field day, a special time when all the 4-H families and their puppies gathered for fun and games. Cinderella romped and played with the other dogs. She caught balls and rolled in the grass. She even sneaked off with a 4-H boy's napkin at the picnic. At first this frightened Benjamin for he knew that the instructors were watching the dogs carefully for signs of bad manners. But Cinderella properly released the napkin when Benjamin patted her head and held out his hand. All in all,

she was a delight and Benjamin was proud of her.

But the field day was also a workday for Cinderella and Benjamin. First Cinderella was checked by a veterinarian. He found her healthy and alert. And beautiful! Her coat had darkened from yellow to a gleaming butterscotch gold. Her eyes were gentle and glowing. And her disposition was pleasant.

Then, while the instructors observed, Benjamin put Cinderella on her leash and led her through a narrow obstacle course. The course was lined with chairs and cans and boxes. Overhead brightly colored balloons, pennants, and streamers danced in the breeze. Most puppies would bark at such a spectacle and would bump their way noisily down the crowded course. But Cinderella walked the length quietly without touching one chair or can or box.

The instructors next shot a pistol behind her and even dropped a heavy metal chair in her path, but Cinderella held her course. Living with a wholesome and kind family had helped her mature and grow self-confident.

"Good girl," Benjamin praised.

"You've done your job well," the instructor told him.

Benjamin was both pleased and sad. He was proud of Cinderella, but the year was flying by. Cinderella was no longer a puppy. Soon she would be ready for school.

THREE
STARTING SCHOOL

One morning a van from the training school arrived to pick up Cinderella. The Weavers tried to be brave as they hugged her and told her good-bye. Benjamin fought back his tears, but Amy cried openly when the trainer coaxed Cinderella into the van and closed the door. Watching longingly, she dashed from window to window. As the van pulled away,Cinderella's face was pressed against the rear window, her ears drooping.

The trainers and instructors at the school welcomed Cinderella warmly. Her first stop was at the veterinary clinic. She was measured and weighed and checked thoroughly. Then she was permitted to play with the other dogs.

The workers understood that Cinderella would miss her family, so they gave her extra love and care. She also had lots of time to play. But by nightfall Cinderella's spirits began to sag. Her tail drooped and her eyes grew sad as she was put into her cage to sleep.

Early the next morning a young man named Rick opened the door of Cinderella's cage. Rick would be her instructor. He had once been a 4-H puppy raiser like Benjamin. Then he spent four years learning to teach guide dogs. Part of his training was done in an unusual way. For two weeks he wore a blindfold and could not see. During this time he used a dog to lead him, just as blind people do. In this way he learned a little about how sightless people feel.

Rick took Cinderella to the training grounds. First he checked her obedience skills. Cinderella ran to the end of the fenced area.

"Cindy," Rick called. The dog perked her ears and looked toward Rick. "Come," the instructor said, patting his leg. Cinderella came bounding back. "Atta girl, Cindy," Rick said enthusiastically.

Then they repeated the lesson.

Rick fastened a leash to Cinderella's collar. "Cindy, sit," he said, pressing his hand against Cinderella's rear. "Atta girl," he praised. Then he taught her a new command she would need in guide work. "Cindy, forward," he commanded, moving his right hand and foot forward. Cinderella obeyed at once. "Good girl," Rick exclaimed. In the same manner Cinderella learned two other new commands, *right* and *left*.

After a few days Cinderella seemed happy again and could follow all commands promptly and correctly. She had earned the right to wear a harness in addition to her leash. A harness has a chest and belly strap for the dog, and a handle for the master. It is much easier to communicate messages between master and dog with a harness. After a while Cinderella would understand that whenever she wore a harness she was at work.

But first she had to "unlearn" a lesson. Ordinarily a dog on leash follows, or *heels*, its master. A guide dog with a harness, however, must lead. But the dog must lead gently to keep from toppling its master.

"Cindy, forward," Rick said and pointed ahead. Cinderella hesitated. "Forward," Rick said, louder than before. Cinderella inched forward uncertainly. "Good girl," Rick said, rubbing her fur. Each time she stepped ahead, Rick praised her. Gradually Cinderella learned the amount of force to apply when leading.

After ten days Cinderella had a new experience. She and Rick went downtown in a van. They spent several hours walking on crowded sidewalks and crossing busy streets. Cinderella made many errors. When she

stepped from a curb without halting, Rick drew her back and tapped the curb with his foot. "Cindy, no, no," he said firmly but kindly, then commanded Cinderella to sit before going forward again. At the next curb he did the same thing. Soon Cinderella learned that she was to pause at every corner so that Rick could feel the curb with his foot before stepping off.

The school had purposely placed a number of obstacles along the way. One was a large garbage can on Rick's side of the sidewalk. Cinderella walked by without brushing it, but Rick bumped into the can with a loud clatter. "Cindy, no, no," he said, slapping the can with his hand. They backed up and tried again. And again. On the fourth try Cinderella led Rick to the center of the sidewalk, well away from the can. "Atta girl, Cindy," Rick said joyously.

In the same way Cinderella also learned to lead Rick around a flower cart, a hot dog stand, and a leaning ladder. Now they went to town regularly. They walked around growling dogs. They went through revolving doors. They rode an elevator. They went into a bank and an office. One afternoon they even went into a coffee shop with a sign on the door reading "No Dogs Allowed." Rick knew that shop and restaurant owners make an exception for guide dogs.

Inside he signaled Cinderella forward slowly among

the tables, using short forward movements of his hand. When Cinderella paused at a table where people were sitting, Rick said, "Cindy, no," and motioned her forward again. Finally they came to an empty table and chair. "Atta girl," he praised Cinderella generously as he firmly patted the table. "Good dog." Now Cinderella would understand that she should search for an empty table for her master. She would also know to look for an empty seat on a bus or a subway, in a schoolroom or at a meeting. While Rick ate his sandwich, Cinderella sat quietly at his feet. She had learned the lessons Benjamin had taught her about not begging.

Once Cinderella led Rick into a heavy lead pipe extending from a truck. Cinderella could walk underneath the pipe, but it hit Rick chest high. This could injure a blind master who could not see the danger. Rick slapped the pipe noisily and corrected Cinderella firmly. By the time that lesson ended, Cinderella knew to look for obstacles taller than she.

Ever since she was a pup, Cinderella had been taught to obey her master's command. Now she had to learn to disobey when necessary, for often there would be danger present that a blind person could not see. That person's life could depend on Cinderella's ability to think for herself.

To teach this difficult lesson, the training school

arranged for a car to screech around the corner just as Cinderella and Rick stepped from the curb. Cinderella stopped in time. In the next block a car crossed their path as it turned into a driveway. Again Cinderella stopped in time.

"Cindy, forward," Rick commanded when the automobile disappeared.

Just as Cinderella stepped out, the car backed into their path again. The dog halted, and again Rick was saved from harm.

Sometimes children would call to Cinderella and watch as she led her master down the street. Because she was wearing a harness and responding carefully to her master's signals, Cinderella paid no attention. But at street corners, while they were awaiting a traffic signal, Rick would answer the children's questions and sometimes would permit them to pet her briefly. It is important for people to know that guide dogs are lovable animals and not machines to do their masters' bidding.

One morning Rick wore a blindfold for their trip into town. From now on, Cinderella would be on her own. She seemed to sense her importance. She was confident and alert, and safely led Rick through all the obstacles in their path.

Three months passed. Half the dogs in Cinderella's

class had already failed and were returned to their 4-H families to live as pets. Cinderella, however, was still doing well. But there was one more test to pass, the biggest test of all.

FOUR
MEETING
A BLIND MASTER

One day sixteen blind people arrived at the training school. They came from all parts of the United States. The youngest was an eighteen-year-old girl named Belveia, a high school senior. Next year she would go away to college and would need a dog to guide her to classes and around the campus. Belveia had never before been away from home alone. Naturally she was frightened.

Belveia shared a room with another blind woman in the school's dormitory. Early the next morning Belveia and the other blind students felt their way down a hall-way to the dining room, where they were led to tables. After breakfast Belveia's work began.

Before she learned to work with a dog, she first had to learn to work with Rick, who played the role of a dog. Practicing with a leash and later with a harness, Belveia learned to command and follow Rick. She learned to use the leash only when she needed to know where the dog was, and to use the harness when the dog was actually leading. When Belveia was sitting, she would place the harness handle on the dog's back and keep only the leash on her lap. When only the collar was worn, the dog would know that it was "off-duty" and could rest or play. Belveia was told to allow plenty of play time for her dog every day.

Rick meanwhile observed Belveia's strength and size and the pace of her walk. He also observed that she was friendly and soft-spoken. She seemed the perfect master for Cinderella.

"Belveia, this is the dog we have chosen for you," Rick said after a few days. "She's a golden retriever and her name is Cinderella. When she is working, her call name will be Cindy."

Belveia reached out to touch her new companion. For a few minutes Cinderella ran back and forth from Rick to Belveia. Each time she returned to Belveia, her new master hugged her affectionately. Cinderella responded with lavish licks of her wet tongue on Belveia's cheeks, ears, and hands.

When Rick saw that a genuine fondness had developed between the two, he handed Belveia a leash and walked away. Belveia attached the leash to Cinderella's collar. At that moment Cinderella began working for a new master, and Belveia was now responsible for her guide dog's care.

That night Cinderella slept beside Belveia's bed, wearing a night chain, a simple chain to keep her from wandering away, attached to a wall hook within her master's reach. Early the next morning Belveia carefully groomed Cinderella with a brush supplied by the school. The trainer brought bowls of food and water, and let Belveia place them in a special feeding area where Cinderella would now eat. Then Belveia followed Cinderella to a paved area outdoors for a "potty break." After Cinderella relieved herself, the trainer scooped up the waste and removed it. Later, after Belveia returned home with Cinderella, she would learn to judge when and where Cinderella had relieved herself by placing her hand on the dog's rear. Then Belveia could use a plastic bag to pick up the waste.

Cinderella led Belveia back indoors and down the hallway to the dining room. At the doorway Belveia paused. The room was filled with chatter and laughter and clinking dishes, and she felt suddenly alone. Would Cinderella abandon her when she saw familiar

staff members and dogs she knew? Would she search for Rick? But Belveia needn't have feared. Cinderella led her safely to a table and sat quietly at her side as Belveia relaxed and joined the others.

Then the hardest work of all began. This time Belveia would train with Cinderella, while Rick stayed close by.

Soon they were ready to go downtown. Rick watched carefully as Cinderella led Belveia down the same streets and through the same buildings where she had led him. They walked five miles or more every day. When they returned to the school, Belveia always remembered to remove the harness and leash, and to permit Cinderella to play with the other dogs or run in the dog run just outside her door.

After three weeks it was time for Cinderella and Belveia to solo. As they stepped from the van, Rick told Belveia the route she should follow.

"Three blocks straight ahead, cross the main boulevard with a median strip in the center, left at the next corner, turn right after two blocks, then find the jewelry store," he said.

Belveia carefully memorized the instructions and repeated them to the trainer.

"Cindy, forward," she commanded, hoping her voice did not shake as much as her knees did.

Up the sidewalk they walked, down curbs, around a

flower box. "Good dog," Belveia said, patting Cinderella's head each time she performed a command.

At intersections Belveia listened carefully to be able to tell when the traffic light changed. Dogs are color-blind and cannot be taught to tell red from green. But even if Belveia gave a signal too early, she knew Cinderella would not budge an inch until the street was clear.

Belveia carefully counted every block they walked and remembered every turn, for she would have to find her way back to the van without help from Rick. "That's block one, Cindy," she said aloud as they paused at the first curb. Guide dogs seem to like being talked to by their masters, and counting blocks aloud helped Belveia to remember. Cinderella was leading her confidently, and a sense of freedom washed over the girl. For the first time she was walking city streets without a cane or a person to help her.

"We're going to be a great team, Cindy," she exclaimed.

When they arrived at the last street, Belveia asked directions to the jewelry store. "It's the third building on the right," she was told. She judged the distance and walked forward. "Cindy, halt," she commanded when she thought she was on target. "Right," she said, moving her hand to the right. Cinderella led her to a door. Belveia felt for the knob, turned it, and she and Cinderella entered.

"Good for you both," Rick's familiar voice rang out. "And it didn't take you long." Rick hugged Belveia. Then they both hugged Cinderella. "Now you'll have to find your way back to the van," Rick said.

Each day Belveia ventured farther from the van. One day Belveia found the drugstore Rick had pointed out. She and Cinderella went inside and bought cards to send home. It took longer than Belveia had expected, and she knew they must rush back to the van.

At the first corner she paused as usual. "Cindy, forward," she commanded as soon as she sensed the traffic light had changed. Cinderella stepped forward, then stopped abruptly. A bicycle swerved noiselessly around the corner, right into the path Belveia would have taken. It came so close that Belveia felt the rush of air against her arms and legs. "Cindy, forward," she said again after taking a moment to regain her confidence. But Cinderella, moving in so close that Belveia could feel the fur against her legs, refused to move. At that second another bike zoomed around the corner, barely missing the curb and the people waiting there. Belveia, of course, did not see either bicycle and could not hear them over the roar of traffic.

"Your dog saved you from harm," an onlooker exclaimed. Belveia stooped and hugged Cinderella longer than she had ever hugged her before.

"Good, good dog," she said. "Thank you, Cindy."

FIVE
GRADUATION

Since graduation day was warm and clear, the ceremony was held outdoors on a patio. Chairs were arranged in rows. The first row was reserved for the new guide-dog masters. The 4-H puppy raisers and their families filled the other seats. Benjamin was already raising another puppy for the school, but he had been invited to Cinderella's graduation.

Before the ceremony was to begin, a trainer led Cinderella away on a leash, and for the first time in four weeks she and Belveia were separated. How strange Belveia felt not to have Cinderella close by. A short while later, an assistant lined up all the blind people who would graduate, and they all marched in, each on the arm of an assistant, and took their seats up front.

Standing on a platform, the director of the school welcomed the visitors and congratulated the students and guide dogs. Then he called each student, one by one, to the stage to receive a dog and to say a few words.

"Congratulations," he said to Belveia when it was her turn. "Both you and Cinderella have done a fine job. You have earned the right to have your own guide dog."

Benjamin led Cinderella to the stage and, smiling broadly, he handed the leash to Belveia. Belveia was so overjoyed that she stooped and hugged Cindy, and Cindy's tail wagged so fiercely that she almost knocked the microphone over. Then the director handed the microphone to Belveia.

"I want to thank the school for giving me new freedom and independence," she said in a soft, clear voice. "And I'd like to thank Benjamin and his family for raising such a fine puppy. But most of all I want to thank Cinderella for being my new eyes. She's the best friend I have ever had."

The audience burst into applause as Belveia again took her seat in the first row. This time Cinderella sat at her feet, ready to obey her new master's commands for the rest of her working life.

SIX
A NEW LIFE

Now it was time for farewells. Belveia and Cinderella soon would be leaving for the airport and a trip across the country. With Cinderella at her side, Belveia told each student good-bye. She felt sad as she hugged her roommate and her roommate's guide dog. "I promise to write," she said.

But the saddest farewell was with Rick. "I can never thank you enough for Cindy and me," she said. But Cinderella was doing her own thanking. Her tail wagging, she licked Rick's hands and nuzzled his knees. When the trainer stooped to hug her, she washed his face and ears with her busy tongue.

"How do you feel?" Rick asked Belveia.

"Sad. Happy. Scared. Excited," Belveia replied. "All of these. It will be such a miracle to go places on my own without asking someone to take me. Thanks to Cindy, I can even go away to college, and my family won't have to worry about me."

"Remember, we'll keep in touch," Rick said. "And we'll visit you and Cindy every year to be sure everything is going well."

"I'm glad we'll be seeing you again," Belveia said, giving Rick a hug.

"The van is here to take you to the airport, Belveia," someone close to the door called out.

The girl stooped to lift the harness handle from Cinderella's back. Immediately the dog's tail stopped wagging, and her eyes grew alert and watchful as she awaited Belveia's signal.

"Cindy, forward," Belveia said, motioning with her hand. Cinderella perked her ears and led her master confidently through the door and into a new life.

A SPECIAL MESSAGE

If you see a guide dog while it is working, you must never speak to it or try to pet it without its master's consent. The dog must concentrate to guard its master from harm and must not be distracted.

Guide-dog training schools have differing rules regarding visitors. It is a good idea to telephone before planning a visit. You can learn the location of training schools by calling your local library or an association for the blind.

For information on puppy raising for guide dogs, you can inquire at your library or write the 4-H Clubs of America, Room 5035S, U.S. Department of Agriculture, Washington, D.C. 20250.

INDEX

Illustrations are <u>underlined</u>.

Belveia, 31
  and Cinderella, 32, <u>33</u>,
    34, <u>35</u>
    caring for, 34
    in dining room with,
      34, 36
    downtown with, 36, <u>37</u>
    saved from harm by, 39,
      <u>40</u>
    soloing with, 36,
      38–39
  graduation of, 41–42, <u>43</u>
  and Rick, 32, 34, 44, <u>45</u>,
    46

Cinderella, 1, <u>2</u>, 7, <u>8</u>, <u>11</u>
  and Belveia, 31–32, <u>33</u>,
    34, <u>35</u>, 36, <u>37</u>, 38–39,
    <u>40</u>, 44, <u>45</u>, 46
    protecting, 39
  birth of, 7
  in coffee shop, 25, <u>26</u>,
    27
  disobeying commands,
    27–28
  downtown, 23, 25, 27, <u>29</u>
  graduation of, 41–42, <u>43</u>
  leading master around
    obstacles, 25, 27

learning commands, 17,
   22–23
misbehaving, 16, 17
nickname of, 9
obedience skills of, 17,
   22
as a puppy, 7, <u>8</u>, 9
reactions to animals by,
   10, <u>11</u>, 16
reflexes of, 9–10
socialization of, 10, 12, 13
temperament of, 9–10
testing of, 9–10, 19
at training school field
   day, 17, <u>18</u>, 19
at Weavers' home, 13,
   <u>14</u>, 15–17, 20

Eustis, Dorothy, 3
Eustis, George, 3

4-H Clubs of America, 12,
   17, 47
Frank, Morris, 3

German shepherd dogs, 3, 4
Germans, 3
golden retrievers, 1, 4, 7
guide-dog training schools, 3–4,
6, 47
funding for, 4
in Switzerland, 3
in United States, 3–4
guide dogs, 1, 3, <u>5</u>
breeds used as, 4
cost of, 4
history of, 1, 3
requirements for, 4
training of, 4, 6
Guide Dogs for the Blind,
   4

harness, 23, <u>24</u>, 28, 32

Labrador retrievers, 4
Leader Dogs, 4

night chain, 34, <u>35</u>

Pilot Dogs, 4
puppy raisers, 10, 12

Rick, 22, <u>24</u>
avoiding obstacles, 25
and Belveia, 32, 34, 44,
   <u>45</u>, 46
blindfolded, 28, <u>29</u>
and bystanders, 28

downtown with Cinderella, 23, 25

teaching commands to Cinderella, 22–23

Seeing Eye, The, 3

Seeing Eye Dogs, 4

socializing, 10, 12, 13

Weaver, Amy, 13, 16, 20

Weaver, Benjamin, 13, 14, 15–17, 19, 20, 27, 41, 42

Weaver, Mrs., 16

World War One, 1